TINY DESERT GARDEN

Your own collection of succulents

Written by Simon Beecroft

BRING THE OUTSIDE IN

A dish garden is an arrangement of miniature plants that can be placed on a desk, shelf or window ledge. These compact collections evoke a spirit of peacefulness and serenity.

The origins of dish gardens are somewhat lost in the mists of time, but the practice may have originated centuries ago in Japan. Landscape gardeners would create miniature models of their work to help customers visualize the end result.

Your dish garden brings together some captivating cacti and stylish succulents – as well as a couple of surprises!

BOTANICAL KNOW-HOW

Succulents are plants with fleshy leaves or stems that store water, allowing them to survive in hot and dry environments. Cacti also have fleshy stems and branches, but with scales or prickles instead of leaves.

From the majestic blue blooms of *Echeveria* "Purple Pearl" to the dangling delights of String of Hearts, your desert garden is bursting with colour and interest. Look deeper and you'll find a four-leaf clover and a tiny ladybird.

When building your model, enjoy the relaxing flow of creation. Feel free to place each mini-plant in the dish as you like. You don't have to follow the instructions exactly. Create your own sense of harmony and let your creativity bloom!

"The perfect garden,
enclose nothing less

no matter its size, should than the entire universe."

Mexican architect and engineer Luis Barragán

PURPLE PEARL

(Echeveria)

Family: *Crassulaceae*
Origin: Semi-desert areas of Central and South America

Echeveria "Purple Pearl" is a glorious evergreen succulent with fleshy grey-lilac leaves that form large, majestic rosettes. Its sculptural form and soothing hues bring a calm elegance to any setting.

Echeveria's ancestors come from the desert landscapes of northeastern Mexico. The species is named after a Mexican botanical illustrator, Atanasio Echeverría y Godoy, who trained at the Royal Art Academy in Mexico. Echeverría explored Mexico and Cuba in the 1780s and 1790s with his sketchbook and box of paints. He created hundreds of exquisite watercolours of botanical life.

Useful tip: Choose a position in your dish garden that allows this eye-catching centrepiece to shine without dominating the smaller plants.

LIME N' CHILE

(Echeveria)

Family: *Crassulaceae*
Origin: Semi-desert areas of Central and South America

Echeveria "Lime n' Chile" is an effortless star. It is striking enough to stand alone but won't steal all the limelight when mingled with other plants to enhance a dish garden's visual appeal.

Most captivating are the symmetrical rosettes of thick, wedge-shaped leaves with their entrancing lime-green hues. Its leaf colour is unique among all the many species of *Echeveria*.

In bright light, the leaf tips can take on hints of red. Throughout the spring and summer, the plant blooms with spicy pink-red bell-shaped flowers (thus the "chile", pronounced "chilli", in its name).

Useful tip: You can choose whether to place both LEGO® *Echeveria* plants next to each other or to separate them using other plants.

BARREL CACTUS
(Echinocactus)

Family: *Cactaceae*
Origin: Deserts of Mexico and the Southwestern USA

Cacti are prominent features of the natural world in Mexican history. They appear in 16th-century Aztec manuscripts and on the flag of Mexico today.

The barrel cactus' ability to thrive in harsh desert conditions makes it a metaphor for resilience and strength. Lost travellers in the desert can use the plant as a compass as it tends to lean toward the south-west. Sometimes, it leans so far that it topples under its own weight!

In summer, bright pink flowers emerge from the top of this extraordinary and fascinating plant.

Useful tip: Choose when to let your LEGO barrel cactus bloom by adding or removing the pink 1×1 round piece.

SNAKE PLANT
(Sansevieria cylindrica)

Family: *Asparagaceae*
Origin: Rocky, arid areas of West Africa

The cylindrical snake plant is unmistakable for its elegant and unique tube-like shape and its long, pointed leaves that can grow to over 1.8 metres tall in the wild.
Its many common names include African spear, dagger fern, bowstring hemp, devil's tongue and lucky plant.

Snake plants are natural air cleansers, helping to remove toxins from the air and improving air quality. These purifying qualities have even been noticed by NASA. The space agency found that just one plant positioned every 9.2 square metres could be enough to efficiently clean the air in a space station.

Useful tip: Get creative in how you position your tiny snake plant to best show off its stylish spines.

STRING OF PEARLS
(Curio rowleyanus)

Family: *Asteraceae*
Origin: Southwest Africa to Namibia

String of Pearls gets its name from the small, round, pearl-like leaves that adorn its long, trailing stems. These spherical leaves are perfectly adapted to help the plant survive in its natural desert environment as they minimize water loss through evaporation.

Named after British botanist Gordon Rowley, this evergreen perennial is part of the daisy family (*Asteraceae*) and is native to dry areas of the Cape of South Africa. String of Pearls is like a living charm bracelet, with each leaf offering a wish for good luck, prosperity and success.

Useful tip: Allow at least one String of Pearls to rest over the tray edge for decorative appeal.

STRING OF HEARTS
(Ceropegia Woodii)

Family: *Apocynaceae*
Origin: Southern Africa

String of Hearts combines the graceful beauty of nature with a touch of fairy-tale enchantment. This hanging succulent has many common names, including rosary vine, hearts-on-a-string and sweetheart vine. Its stems are wire-thin, with beautiful grey-green leaves that hang off them like charms. Shaped like hearts, these leaves, together with the twisting, trailing stems, seem to tell a tale of life's twists and turns.

In the wild, String of Hearts is found on stony hillsides across southern Africa and in parts of Madagascar. It can reach lengths of over 3.5 metres. After the rainy season, the plant produces an abundance of flowers.

Useful tip: Allow your String of Hearts to cascade over the edge of the dish. Position it off-centre for a more natural look.

LUCKY CLOVER

(Trifolium)

Family: *Fabaceae*
Origin: Europe and Central Asia

Count yourself lucky if you find a four-leaf clover: they are very rare and are said to bring good fortune to the finder. Only one in an estimated 5,000 clovers have four leaves (most have just three). Even rarer are those with five or more leaves. The record number of leaves on a single clover is 63!

Four-leaf clovers are said to ward off bad luck. In some traditions, the four leaves have symbolic meanings: faith, hope, love and luck. In medieval times, children believed carrying a four-leaf clover would enable them to see fairies. Want to increase your luck? It is said that if you pass your four-leaf clover on to someone else, your luck will double.

Useful tip: Hide your clovers beneath the petals of another plant so they can be "discovered".

LADYBIRD

(Coccinella septempunctata)

Family: *Coccinellidae*
Origin: Europe, Asia and Africa

"Ladybird, ladybird, fly away home ..."

This children's rhyme is often recited while gently blowing the insect from the hand or clothing and making a wish. The shiny, red seven-dotted variety is just one of more than 5,000 different species of ladybirds beetle found around the world. Some species have just two spots, while others have 16. Some ladybirds have stripes or even no markings at all.

Many cultures consider ladybirds to be good luck. Farmers and gardeners especially love them, since they consume aphids and other plant-destroying insects.

Useful tip: Your ladybird can hide among the plants or even come to rest on top of one of them.

Follow the steps to build your Tiny Desert Garden.

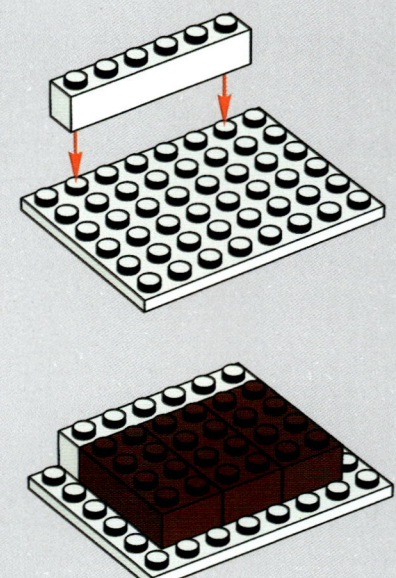

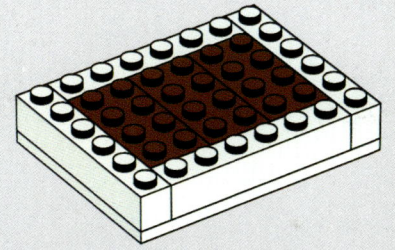

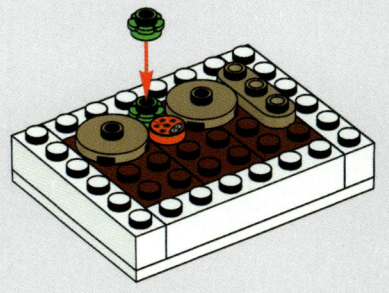

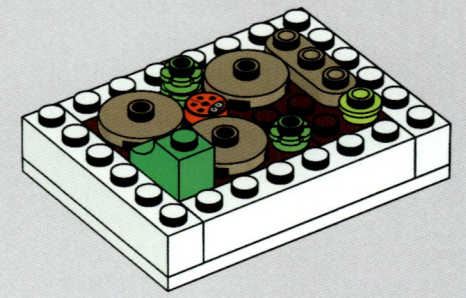

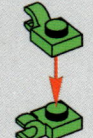

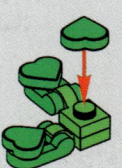

Editor Simon Beecroft
Designer Piotr Paczkowski

For LEGO Publishing
Editor Ashley Blais
Visual Designers Nina Koopmann and Martin Leighton Lindhardt

Your opinion matters

Please scan this QR code to give feedback to help us enhance your future experiences